POST-WAR KILMARNOCK

FRANK BEATTIE

This book is dedicated to my children; from left, Grant, Rosie and Fraser. Scotland's future will soon be in the hands of their generation... and Scotland's future is bright.

First published 2008

The History Press Ltd.
The Mill, Brimscombe Port
Stroud, Gloucestershire, GL5 2QG
www.thehistorypress.co.uk

© Frank Beattie, 2008

Reprinted in 2009, 2011

The right of Frank Beattie to be identified as the Author
of this work has been asserted in accordance with the
Copyrights, Designs and Patents Act 1988.

British Library Cataloguing in Publication Data.
A catalogue record for this book is available from the British Library.

ISBN 978 0 7509 5038 1

Typesetting and origination by The History Press Ltd.
Printed in Great Britain

Contents

Some familiar faces. Clockwise from top left: Robert Burns, John Wilson, acrobat 1, acrobat 2, swimmer 1, swimmer 2, acrobat 3, acrobat 4 and centre, Jimmie Shaw. *(Frank Beattie)*

Introduction

Shortly before midnight on 5 June 1944, Joe MacGregor was taking part in the early stages of the biggest military operation in history. Joe was born in Kilmarnock and brought up in Lawson Street. When he was still young, Joe's family migrated to America. In 1944 he was one of the pathfinders who would land in Normandy and clear the way for the paratroopers who were to secure the causeways and the dry land so that the D-Day invasion could proceed.

Joe was one of the first allied men to land in enemy-held territory. D-Day heralded the start of the closing stages of the Second World War. This Longest Day brought peace nearer.

It took a while for the world to start to recover from the war. Many families lost family members, and not all in military service. Civilians in Kilmarnock escaped lightly. The town suffered just one air raid with only four casualties. Not so far away, Clydebank suffered the heaviest bombing in Britain. Only three buildings were left undamaged by the Luftwaffe.

The peace having been won, the country faced many high priority tasks. As soldiers, sailors and airmen came home, they had to adjust from military to civilian work. Production in the factories had to be switched back to suit civilian needs rather than those of the military. Houses fit for heroes had once again to be provided. The task was enormous and it would take years, even decades, to complete.

There was a new social order. Railways, road transport, electricity, gas and coal mining were all transferred into state ownership. Homes for the elderly were provided by local councils. For the rest of the 1940s many goods remained rationed.

But there was a mood of optimism. The late 1940s and '50s saw industry start to recover and new industries like Glacier Metal and Massey-Harris were enticed to come to Kilmarnock. A massive house-building programme was started, creating a new community at Shortlees.

The 1960s was a decade of optimism and as prosperity increased, so did car ownership. This led to a reassessment of how towns like Kilmarnock should cope with a massive increase in road traffic and a sharp decline in railways as the Beeching cuts saw many local lines and stations closed. There was also more house building and another community was created at Bellfield.

The 1970s was a decade of rapid change. Centralisation began to creep in, even at local authority level, and in 1974 the first elections were held for the new Kilmarnock and Loudoun District Council and for Strathclyde Regional Council. These replaced various town and district councils in the Kilmarnock and Irvine Valley area.

In local government, many smaller towns lost their own local councils. Kilmarnock became the local authority centre for nearby towns such as Stewarton,

Galston, Newmilns and Darvel. Prosperity and expansion were the key words, at least until inflation started to escalate and unemployment began to climb. Even so, it was too late to stop plans that had already been set in motion. Much of the core of Kilmarnock was demolished. All the charm of more than 200 years of architecture and character was swept aside and replaced by what could only be described as 'shoe-box architecture'.

The decline which had begun in the 1970s accelerated, driven by a political philosophy that saw the closure of many of Kilmarnock's traditional heavy industries. As the old industries waned, nothing replaced them. In 1986 unemployment in the Kilmarnock area peaked at 19.1 per cent and many people blamed one woman and her political philosophy.

Recovery was difficult but with it came the new age of high technology in an era predicted in the 1960s by Arthur C. Clarke, who coined the term 'global village'. Suddenly, everyone was using computers. New technologies brought new opportunities and new businesses that were all part of global corporations. At least the dirt and the grime of the old heavy industries were mostly gone.

There were more changes in local government. The 1970s' system had never been popular and in 1996 the two-tier system was replaced by single-tier authorities. Kilmarnock came under East Ayrshire Council, which had responsibilities for education, social work, leisure, planning and other services.

But the biggest political change of the 1990s came with recalling the Scottish Parliament which had 'adjourned' its last meeting in 1707, giving Scotland the chance at last to develop policies more suited to its needs.

The dawn of the new millennium brought another major change in Kilmarnock. The long, and at times bitter campaign to get a motorway built between Kilmarnock and Glasgow was finally won and as journey times to the city centre were cut, more and more people began commuting from Kilmarnock to Glasgow. The result has been an unprecedented housing boom, with thousands of new homes being built in and around Kilmarnock and many more thousands planned for the coming decade.

Kilmarnock, it seems, has at least recovered from the gloom of the decline of old industries. There is a new confidence in the town and in the country which is reflected not only in the building work that is going on all around town, but also in a new pride which is now being taken in our streets and parks.

Frank Beattie, 2008

Crowds gather for the official opening of the Burns shopping centre in 1976. *(Frank Beattie)*

1

The Coming of Peace

It is only the dead who have seen the end of war. (Plato)

Kilmarnock's War Memorial was built in the form of a temple and dedicated in 1927 to the local men who died 'for king and country' in the First World War. After the Second World War, more plaques were added with the names of the dead from this war and, later still, the names of local men killed in the Korean War. *(Frank Beattie)*

The war against Japan was still going on when the European conflict ended. Many of the children in this VE-Day picture (thought to have been taken in Elderslie Crescent) would not have been able to remember a time of peace. *(Derry Martin)*

At the start of 1944, the British Special Air Service (SAS) which had been a special force for much of the war, was brought up to brigade strength and was based in Ayrshire for training in preparation for D-Day, carried out with similar forces from France and Belgium. Among other places, they used Loudoun Castle, Bellfield House, Dankeith House and the Kilmarnock swimming pool, which had a unique wave-making machine. This memorial is at Darvel. *(Frank Beattie)*

e original mansion house Springhill was built in 40 and was home to the nie family who made their une from local coal mines. 1945 the last of the local nies left the house to the ple of Kilmarnock to be d as an eventide home. 1966 sheltered houses in grounds were officially ned and named Springhill dens. In 2007 ambitious ns were announced for a jor expansion of the original nsion. *(Frank Beattie)*

Mount House was built as a private residence in 1793 and remained in the hands of the Guthrie family for several generations. In 1950 it was bought by Kilmarnock Town Council along with 68 acres of land. It was opened as a home for the elderly in 1953. It was closed in 1996 and today much of the land around the mansion is used for housing. *(Frank Beattie)*

In 1950 the town council agreed to lease Annanhill House in Irvine Road to the Massey-Harris tractor company for use as their workers' social club. The house had been bought by the town in 1929 and the grounds were a popular place for walks. Today the house has been converted into flats. *(Frank Beattie)*

The mansion house of Bellsford Bank in Richardland Road was at one time one of the family homes of the Paxton family who ran a nearby brewery. In 1950 it was renamed Bellsford House when it became a children's home. The running of the home passed from Kilmarnock Town Council to Strathclyde Regional Council and later back to more local control through East Ayrshire Council, who continue to provide excellent care on the premises. *(Frank Beattie)*

Richardland House in Bentinck Street was originally built in about 1820 as the home of the Paxton family. Their brewery was adjacent to the house. From about 1922 to roughly 1947 it was a private nursing home and in 1950 it was bought by the hydraulic engineering firm of Glenfield and Kennedy for use as a guest house. In the 1970s the house was demolished to make way for a printing company. *(Frank Beattie)*

The mansion of Tankerha in London Road was originally a private home, but in 1950 it was opened as a Church of Scotland home for up to twenty-two children. It operated as such for thirty years, closing in 1980. The building is today private residences. *(Kilmarnock Standard)*

BLAIR AVENUE, HURLFORD

In 1945 the urgent need for new houses began to be met with projects to build council houses. Among the first to be completed were those at Blair Avenue in Hurlford, and at Irvine Road, Kilmarnock Road and Playingfield Road in Crosshouse. As shortages of manpower and materials resulting from the war eased, council house building was soon to reach new heights. *(Frank Beattie)*

To cope with post-war housing needs, Kilmarnock Town Council embarked on an ambitious twenty-five-year programme of house building which would see 10,000 council homes built between 1947 and 1972. This programme involved vast new housing areas on what had previously been green space. *(Frank Beattie)*

Shortlees was one of the first of the major new housing areas to be built around Kilmarnock. New communities need more than just houses and in 1953, Shortlees Church was opened for worship. It is a plain building reflecting the shortages of the time. *(Frank Beattie)*

To provide for the needs of the children from the new Shortlees area, Shortlees School was opened in 1952. At first it was a junior secondary school, but it later became a primary school. In 2007, the 55-year-old building was replaced by a new school. *(Frank Beattie)*

Left: Perhaps the biggest social change in the immediate post-war years was the programme of nationalisation. The key targets were power and transport, which had a profound impact on various Kilmarnock industries. Gas was first supplied to Kilmarnock by a local private company in 1823. In 1871 the gas company was taken over by the town council. *(Frank Beattie)*

Below: Plans to build an electric power station in Kilmarnock sparked a long and bitter public versus private debate. In the end, the power station which opened in 1904 was run by the town council. Electricity generation was one of the industries taken into state ownership in the 1940s. *(Frank Beattie)*

Scotland's railway revolution started in Kilmarnock in 1812 when a timetabled passenger service operated between Kilmarnock and Troon. Railway services remained in the hands of private companies until the 1940s nationalisation. *(Frank Beattie)*

Road haulage and bus services were also nationalised. In 1948 the Midland bus group moved their garage and engineering operation from Townholm to Nursery Avenue. Midland had been part of the Western SMT since its formation in 1932 but retained its own garage facilities. Scottish Transport had established its garage and engineering works at Nursery Avenue in the 1920s, before the formation of Western SMT. *(Frank Beattie)*

It is perhaps surprising that the government of the late 1940s did not nationalise the banks and other financial institutions. In Scotland, the commercial banks were, and still are, allowed to issue their own notes. *(Royal Bank of Scotland)*

In the years following the end of the Second World War, Norman Archer and his wife set up a shop for the sale and repair of radios, giving it the name of a popular war-time wireless programme, *The Radio Doctor*. As radio work dried up, the shop diversified into selling toys, and in the 1950s and '60s was known to just about every child in Kilmarnock. *(Radio Doctor)*

In 1952, Jim Donald of Galston started an electrical business with capital of £200 and a garden hut for his business premises. Fifty-five years on and trading as J.H. Donald, the business has shops in five Ayrshire towns and is the largest independent electrical trader in the area. *(Frank Beattie)*

As peace returned to the world, the local family business of Browning the baker was established in Kilmarnock in 1945. The business continues to thrive. In 2003, the firm was named British Baker of the Year in the Baking Industry Awards in London and in 2004 they took over the long established Irvine bakery business of John Short & Sons. At this time Shorts had four shops in Irvine and Troon. *(Bob Murray)*

One of the old established retail traders now lost was that of drysalter John Boyle, whose distinctive shop in King Street is seen here from an earlier period. *(Frank Beattie)*

With a generous government grant, Glacier Metal moved to a new site at Riccarton in 1947 on the land of the former Kirkstyle coal pit. The company had moved from London to a temporary factory in Kilmarnock in 1942 to escape possible damage from air raids. *(Frank Beattie)*

With the help of generous government grants, Massey-Harris, later Massey-Ferguson, established a tractor assembly plant at Moorfield Industrial Estate on the edge of Kilmarnock in 1949. The company, which built tractors and combined harvesters, would grow rapidly to become one of the major employers in the area. *(Frank Beattie)*

Left: In the early 1950s Kilmarnock swimmer Margaret McDowall dominated women's international swimming. She won both the Junior and Senior British Championships on successive days when she was just 14, and in 1951, at the first ever international swimming event to be held at Kilmarnock, she helped Scotland win the Bologna Trophy. This picture shows Margaret setting off for the Helsinki Olympics in 1952, when she brought home a silver medal. *(Stewart McLaughlan)*

Below: Golf is important in Ayrshire and Kilmarnock's first municipal golf course was opened in 1909 at Caprington. A second municipal course was built in 1957 in the grounds of Annanhill House. *(Author's collection)*

ANNANHILL GOLF COURSE, KILMARNOCK   D 3787

Cricket has never had the popularity of football, but Kilmarnock has had, and still has a strong cricket side. In 1946 Kilmarnock Cricket Club won the Western Union Championship. Here, young Kilmarnock fans of the sport are given a lesson by England's cricket legend, Len Hutton. *(Stewart McLaughlan)*

The immediate post-war years were dominated by repairs and shortages, but by 1951 the country was ready to mark the dawn of a new era with a Festival of Britain. Many voluntary and commercial organisations took part in a variety of local celebrations and events for the festival. These included a parade of floats displaying Kilmarnock's diverse industries and a march past of members of voluntary groups from around Kilmarnock. *(Stewart McLaughlan)*

In 1953 the A1 bus service started using a new stance in the St Marnock Street car park which served as their main Kilmarnock terminus until they moved to the corner of Cheapside Street and John Dickie Street, pictured above in 1959. Today A1, like Western SMT, is part of the Stagecoach group. *(Frank Beattie)*

Kilmarnock Burgh police force was short of space in Kilmarnock and in 1954 a new administrative headquarters was opened in a former private house at Dundonald Road. The burgh police station was at Sturrock Street and the country police station, serving rural areas, had a station in Bank Street. Today, policing operates from a single station in St Marnock Street. *(Frank Beattie)*

In the 1950s and '60s, Kilmarnock was a vibrant shopping centre with the majority of the shops run as family businesses. One of the main shopping areas was Portland Street, seen here in a postcard from 1950. *(Author's collection)*

Duke Street was opened up in 1859 as the entrance to the town from the east, linking the Cross to London Road. It consisted of fine architecture as well as a good selection of shops. The street was demolished in the 1970s to make way for the Burns shopping centre. *(Author's collection)*

King Street has been the town's foremost shopping area since 1804. The house on the right in the foreground was a doctor's surgery which was demolished soon after this picture was taken. *(Author's collection)*

Few inventions had as much social impact in the second half of the twentieth century as television. Television programmes were broadcast to people in the Kilmarnock area for the first time by the BBC in 1952 and the Coronation in 1953 gave a huge boost to television sales. *(Ayrshire Wireless Ltd)*

2

1960s: The Decade of Music

Imagine all the people, sharing all the world. (John Lennon)

The 1960s was a period of turmoil for many churches, with old buildings being closed, some congregations merging and new churches being built. In 1965, members of the Church of Jesus Christ of Latter Day Saints (commonly referred to as the Mormons), opened their new church building in Whatriggs Road, Bellfield. *(Frank Beattie)*

Bellfield was being built up as a new housing area in the 1960s and with the houses came churches, schools and shops, such as these along Whatriggs Road. *(Frank Beattie)*

St Nininan's Church, also in Bellfield, was opened for Christian worship in 1959. Their first minister was Revd J. Wilkie. *(Frank Beattie)*

This building in Portland Road was opened in 1859 when the congregation of the Gallows Knowe Church relocated owing to their need for bigger and better premises. *(Author's collection)*

The old Howard Church in Portland Road was demolished in 1969 to make way for a new Howard St Andrew's Church, which opened for worship in 1971. *(Frank Beattie)*

In 1966 King Street Church, which had been built in 1832 on the corner of King Street and St Marnock Street, was demolished to make way for a row of shops. *(Stewart McLaughlan)*

Glencairn School was opened in 1876 and extended in 1898 and 1942. In 1960 the old Glencairn Primary School in Low Glencairn Street was closed and most of the children moved to Bentinck Primary School. The Gothic-style building was soon demolished. *(Bob Murray)*

Former railway company houses at Barleith, known as the Barleith Blocks, had been built by the Glasgow and South Western Railway Company (G&SWR) for workers and their families. They were demolished in 1964. The Beeching cuts of 1964 saw the closure of various railway lines, stations and other facilities. The G&SWR main depot at Barleith continued to operate until 1966. *(Stewart McLaughlan)*

By the middle of the 1960s, new council house building was going on in many parts of the town. These flats at West Netherton Street are typical of the period. *(Frank Beattie)*

Towards the end of the 1960s, construction work started on Kilmarnock's biggest housing area yet at New Farm Loch. Eventually the area would encompass thousands of new homes, along with schools, churches, shops and other facilities. *(Frank Beattie)*

Left: In 1964 Kilmarnock Football Club won one of the most sensational games in Scottish football history. They were 3–0 down to Eintracht in the first leg match in the Fair Cities tournament. The second leg was played at Rugby Park and after just 90 seconds, Eintracht scored, taking them 4–0 up on aggregate, but 'Killie' fought back and won the home game 5–1, 5–4 on aggregate. They made front page news in Scotland and Germany. *(Kilmarnock Football Club)*

Below: After one of the most sensational seasons in Kilmarnock Football Club's history, 'Killie' won the 1964/5 Scottish League Championship by a whisker. *(Stewart McLaughlan)*

Members of Portland Bowling Club celebrated the club's centenary in 1960. The Club was founded in 1860, mainly by local businessmen. Early supporters included Provost Archibald Finnie; postmaster David Rankin; locomotive designer Patrick Stirling; coalmaster Peter Sturrock, and other prominent men from the business community in Kilmarnock. *(Frank Beattie)*

The *Kilmarnock Standard* celebrated its centenary in 1963. The paper's first edition in June 1863 carried a mix of local, national and even some international news. In this picture, a copy of the centenary edition is checked by foreman printer Willie McAllister as it comes off the press. *(Stewart McLaughlan)*

In 1964 the Beeching cuts saw the closure of various local railway lines and stations, including services between Kilmarnock and Darvel and between Kilmarnock and Irvine. This move in turn saw the closure of stations at Barleith, Galston, Newmilns and Darvel. Stations at Springside, pictured, and Dreghorn were also closed, as were the goods stations at Kilmaurs, Crosshouse and Gatehead. *(John Hall)*

In the 1960s Portland Street was still a thriving shopping area, and crucial to that success was the location of the town's bus station, seen on the left of this picture. *(Author's collection)*

Above & below: Shopping began to change in the 1960s as more local shops were replaced by national groups. Boots, Marks and Spencer and Woolworths were all established in King Street in the 1920s and '30s, but throughout the 1960s, the trend continued faster than ever before. In 1966, one-way traffic was introduced and later the street was made traffic free. *(Author's collection)*

Before the wholesale destruction of other parts of the town centre, one half of Bank Place, between Bank Street and John Finnie, was cleared for a new branch of the Royal Bank of Scotland. *(Bob Murray)*

Glencairn Square was opened in 1765 and until the twentieth century was known as Holm Square. Many changes have been made over the years, though the buildings in this picture are still recognisable. *(Author's collection)*

The building prominent in the foreground of this picture was the Empire Cinema, originally opened as the Empire Theatre in 1913. One endearing feature was the back row, which comprised of double seats for those who liked a little intimacy. The building was destroyed by fire in 1965. *(Author's collection)*

Hurlford Road. While planning the layout of the Bellfield housing area, Kilmarnock Town Council took the innovative step of attempting to seperate traffic and people. The result won the town a Civic Trust award in 1960. *(Frank Beattie)*

Bellfield House had been given to the people of Kilmarnock by the Buchanan family in 1875 and had been a popular place to visit. After years of neglect and lack of maintenance, it was demolished. Part of the gardens remain as woodland and the area is still popular with walkers. *(Author's collection)*

In the 1960s Kilmarnock still had many engineering companies who were major employers. Kilmarnock Technical College was opened in 1966 to provide courses for those who would take employment in these companies. As employment patterns changed, the building's name was changed to Kilmarnock College and today plans are in hand to relocate the building. *(Frank Beattie)*

Even into the 1960s, it was the custom for most employers to give their workers two weeks off at the same time. This photograph was taken at the Kilmarnock Fair. Originally the fair was known as the Grozet Fair and workers had time off from their employment to help with fruit harvests, particularly the grozets or gooseberries. In the 1960s it was still traditional for Kilmarnock folk to head off to Blackpool in fleets of buses. *(Stewart McLaughlan)*

Towards the end of the 1960s, the pattern of emerging new businesses had changed. Emphasis was now on attracting established companies to set up in town. In 1968 Jaeger came to Kilmarnock and set up a temporary factory making clothes. The business soon expanded in Kilmarnock. *(Gordon Robb)*

T.F. Campbell was a typical local shop. Apart from being a record shop, they also provided toys, prams, bicycles and just about anything that the proprietor fancied selling. Shopping patterns began to change in the 1960s, though the considerable impact the new supermarkets and multinationals would have wasn't quite recognised at the time. *(S&UN)*

Before the advent of the supermarkets, much of the general grocery shopping was done at corner shops. While many such shops have now disappeared, some survive and continue to provide a friendly and more personal alternative to the bigger stores. *(Frank Beattie)*

3

1970s: In with the New

We are the music makers and we are the dreamers of dreams. (Arthur O'Shaughnessy)

It seemed that as the 1970s came in, there was new building work going on all over the town and the country. It wasn't just buildings that were new. Decimal currency was introduced in 1971, followed by the metric system. Just about everything that had been known for generations was about to change. *(Frank Beattie)*

The Cross was the hub of the town with six streets converging there. All six streets had their own character, but in the early 1970s work started on clearing many of the properties to make way for new developments. *(Frank Beattie)*

This was Fore Street before the area was cleared to make way for the new Foregate and a multi-storey car park. *(Sam Ewing)*

The old transport station in Portland Street, above, was opened in 1923 and was one of the first custom-built bus stations in Scotland. Both this bus station and the one in Cheapside Street were replaced by a new station, pictured below, at Green Street in 1974. The new bus station is attached to the Burns shopping centre and serves all the local bus companies. *(Frank Beattie)*

Above & below: Duke Street was opened up in 1859 as the new entrance to the town from the east, linking the Cross and London Road. The distinctive and impressive architecture reflected the confidence of the day. Duke Street was demolished in 1973 to make way for the Burns shopping mall. *(Author's collection and Frank Beattie)*

Right: The new Burns shopping centre was opened in 1976 and given the name Burns Precinct. This was so unpopular that the name was soon changed to the Burns Mall. The centre was bland but functional. However, later changes both inside and out have gone a long way to improve the appearance of the centre. *(Frank Beattie)*

Below: The new Foregate shopping centre officially opened in 1974. This street replaced Fore Street, which had previously replaced the Foregait. *(Frank Beattie)*

The Burns mall was opened in 1976, replacing several of the old twisting streets with what was considered a modern indoor shopping mall. *(Frank Beattie)*

In 1975 a multi-storey car park was opened at the Foregate. At the time it was planned to be the first of several built around the core of the town, but today it remains the only one. *(Frank Beattie)*

Left: Cheapside Street was opened up around the middle of the sixteenth century. This 1973 picture shows one of the old buildings lost during the redevelopment of Kilmarnock town centre. The demolition of this rare example of late seventeenth or early eighteenth-century Scottish domestic architecture was controversial, but went ahead in 1980. *(Frank Beattie)*

Below left: Another controversial loss in the 1970s redevelopment of the town was this property in Market Lane. The building was referred to as Begbie's by Robert Burns in his poem, *The Ordination.* With the construction of King Street in 1804, Begbie's was no longer on the main street. It was advertised for sale in 1816 when it had stabling for twenty-four horses. In the 1970s the property was the side entrance to Woolworths. *(Frank Beattie)*

Below right: After the redevelopment of the former Fore Street area into the Foregate, an area at the top of the new street was named Square of Ales in honour of Ales, Kilmarnock's twin town in France. *(Frank Beattie)*

Some popular pubs were lost in the 1970s redevelopment programme. These included the Bellfield Tavern (which was replaced by the New Bellfield Tavern close to the original site) and the Tam o' Shanter, a popular town centre pub which was not replaced. *(Bob Murray and Frank Beattie)*

Sturrock Street, 1972. This picture was taken as the demolition of the core of the town was about to get under way. Photographed from the Academy Steps, it shows demolition work being carried out on the Plaza Cinema to make way for an extended Marks and Spencer. *(Stewart McLaughlan)*

It was not only the area in the immediate town centre that went through changes at this time. This photograph shows areas in flux around the River Irvine. Land used by industry, particularly Glenfield and Kennedy, is undergoing change, as seen on the left-hand side of the photograph, while on the right, houses are being cleared. *(Stewart McLaughlan)*

It was out with the old nineteenth-century homes and in with more modern houses in many areas of the town. The 1970s flats at Bellsland Place, above, are part of the Robertson Place development area, while these rather odd-shaped houses in Bonnyton Road, below, were quickly nicknamed the Toblerone homes. *(Frank Beattie)*

Drew Keachie was the driving force behind the formation in 1970 of the Kilmarnock Youth Band, which later changed its name to Kilmarnock Concert Brass. In 1978 they won the title of 'Scottish Band of the Year' and in 1979 the title of 'Champion Band of Scotland'. *(Bill Paton)*

There was a royal presence in the town when Queen Elizabeth, Queen of Scots, paid an official visit to Kilmarnock. She was treated to a civic reception at the Dick Institute and was met by Provost Jimmie Mackie. *(Stewart McLaughlan)*

Left & below: The old burgh police station at Sturrock Street was opened in 1898 and had also served as the District Court. The building was demolished in 1973. Police operated from Bank Street until a new divisional headquarters for the Strathclyde Police U Division was officially opened in St Marnock Street in 1978. *(Frank Beattie)*

Above: The old Kilmarnock Grammar School stood on this site from 1877, though it could trace its origins back to at least 1817. In 1975 the building was closed and staff and pupils were transferred to the new Gargieston School at the opposite end of Dundonald Road. Houses were soon built on the old school site and the development took the name of Waterside Court. *(Frank Beattie)*

Right: The 1970s redevelopment saw the relocation of some banks which tended to occupy the most prestigious buildings in the town centre. In 1975 the Clydesdale Bank moved to new property at the Foregate. *(Frank Beattie)*

Andrew Fisher (1862–1928) found work in the local coal pits at the age of 12. Before he was 20 he was agitating for better pay and conditions for miners. He eventually left Scotland for a new life in Australia but continued his interest in politics. He later became Prime Minister of Australia. In 1979 a memorial garden was created in the village of Crosshouse to mark his life and work. Pictured above is Peggy Fisher, daughter of Andrew Fisher, with Sir Gordon Freeth, the London-based Commissioner to Australia. *(Gordon Robb)*

To mark the end of the old Kilmarnock Burgh Council and the start of the new Kilmarnock and Loudoun District Council, the Freedom of the Burgh was awarded to three prominent citizens. Provost Maisie Garven presented the honour to Lord Howard de Walden, Canon Mathew Littleton and statesman Willie Ross. *(Stewart McLaughlan)*

History is vague on the origins of Dean Castle but it is known to have been the seat of the feudal lords of Kilmarnock from about the twelfth century. The castle was substantially damaged by a fire in 1735 and fell into ruin, but it was restored in the twentieth century. In 1975, the 9th Lord Howard de Walden gave Dean Castle and its nationally important collections of musical instruments, tapestries and medieval armaments to Kilmarnock and Loudoun District Council for the use of the people of Kilmarnock. Today the castle with its surrounding country park is a popular visitor attraction. *(Frank Beattie)*

In 1976, the town lost another landmark when the old Kilmarnock power station cooling towers on the bank of the River Irvine were demolished by controlled explosions. One of them was built in 1939 and the other in 1942. *(Frank Beattie)*

In 1976, James Hamilton High School moved from London Road to a new building in Sutherland Drive, pictured above, at the same time becoming James Hamilton Academy. Today the former James Hamilton building in London Road serves as the head offices of East Ayrshire Council. *(Mike Bisset)*

Not all the old town centre streets were demolished. One that survived was Bank Street which retains its own special old-world charm, here given a touch of atmosphere by being photographed in a snowstorm. *(Frank Beattie)*

One curiosity of the 1970s upheaval was Waterloo Street post office, which was opened in 1967 to replace the Duke Street office. When Waterloo Street was demolished, the post office relocated to the Foregate in 1974. However, it retains the name of a street now gone. *(Frank Beattie)*

The corner of Portland Street and Cheapside Street was included in the redevelopment of the town centre. New buildings and changing times attracted national traders to replace local ones. *(Frank Beattie)*

One custom lost in local government reform was that of placing two special lamps outside the provost's home and retaining one of them after the term of office was over. The lamps pictured here in Samson Avenue are outside the home of Provost Annie Mackie. *(Frank Beattie)*

The bridge over the Kilmarnock Water links West Shaw Street and McLelland Drive. It was originally built in 1888 and was one of the town features which escaped the attention of the 1970s planners. *(Frank Beattie)*

4

1980s: Out with the Old

Should auld acquaintance be forgot and never brought to mind? (Robert Burns)

Just as the 1970s seemed to be a period of rapid change and a time for new development, the 1980s was a time for the decline of traditional industries. While some new industries came in, they were not enough to offset a sharp rise in unemployment in the Kilmarnock area, which peaked at 19.1 per cent in 1986. *(Frank Beattie)*

Glenfield and Kennedy was a major employer in Kilmarnock and exported pumps and other hydraulic equipment all over the world. Pictured is an aerial view of their extensive Kilmarnock works. Like so many other industries, it was hit hard by the recession. *(Glenfield and Kennedy)*

Valve making continued to be extensive into the 1980s. *(Kilmarnock Standard)*

Only a small part of the Glenfield business remains in Kilmarnock today but even in the new millennium the company can produce massive valves. However, much of what the company once produced is now in museums. *(Glenfield and Kennedy)*

Above: Kilmarnock had a long tradition of shoe making, even when the industry was a cottage craft. At the start of the twentieth century, the dominant boot and shoe maker was Saxone. Although the business built up a chain of shops, it could not compete against cheap foreign imports and in the middle of the 1980s, the main factory site was cleared to make way for a leisure centre. *(Frank Beattie)*

Left: Another of Kilmarnock's main industries to be hit hard was the carpet makers, BMK. Like Saxone, BMK was founded in Kilmarnock and had a reputation at home and abroad for high quality. Once again, it was cheap imports which hit the company hard and resulted in contraction. The company's main building in West Shaw Street, left, and in Burnside Street, opposite, were demolished. *(Gordon Robb and Frank Beattie)*

John Barr:
it's smootherr by farr.

Above & opposite: Kilmarnock's best-known product is Johnnie Walker whisky. In 1977, a row blew up between the company and the Common Market over pricing, and Red Label, the world's top selling Scotch, was taken off the British market. It was replaced in 1978 by a blend named John Barr. But in 1983, Johnnie Walker Red Label whisky was put back on sale in Britain. (*Diageo*)

RED LABEL returns to the U.K. after 6 YEARS!

Welcome news for Scotch Drinkers

Having been absent returns to
from the Home Market Christmas
Don

One of the most devastating blows of the period came in 1980 when tractor and combined harvester builders, Massey-Ferguson, closed their Kilmarnock plant with the loss of 1,500 jobs. In 1949, the firm had been enticed to Kilmarnock with generous grants. The closure was one of the most severe blows Kilmarnock industry has ever suffered. With the closure, Massey-Ferguson helped set up Moorfield Manufacturing, which gave work to just 200 former employees. *(Massey-Ferguson)*

Another closure was that of the long-established Strang's Foundry in Hurlford. In 1971, the company made the six-bladed propeller required for the restoration of the SS *Great Britain*. But in the coming years work dried up and the business closed. The last propeller to be maufactured was moved out of the factory and placed at Hurlford Cross as a memorial to a lost industry. *(Frank Beattie)*

It was not all contraction in the 1980s. While industries were cutting back, national retailers were keen to expand and in many cases this meant clearing town centre houses. One of the residential streets to be cleared was Kennedy Street. *(Frank Beattie)*

The clearing of land that had been used for housing and by some of the large industries allowed the development of smaller businesses in areas like Glencairn Industrial Estate, which developed from 1984. *(Frank Beattie)*

Kilmarnock had a long tradition of brick-making and stone quarrying. These businesses also made chimney pots, garden ornaments and features for public parks. In 1981 the last part of Armitage Shanks closed their Kilmarnock pottery. The site was soon cleared for housing. However, some of the local parks retain stone lions as silent reminders of that industry. This one is in the Dean Country Park and is being shown off by Rosie Beattie. *(Frank Beattie)*

As part of a concerted effort to attract new businesses, some disused properties were converted for other uses. This former Saxone building was converted into the Netherton Business Centre in 1984. The building at the corner of High Glencairn Street and West Netherton Street provided accommodation for small businesses. *(Frank Beattie)*

Sport in the communities was an important part of the local philosophy and in 1985 the Hunter
Centre, a community and sports centre, was opened at Ardbeg Avenue by Councillor John
Hunter Senior. The centre was named after him in recognition of his twenty-one years as a local
councillor. *(Gordon Robb)*

What was intended to be a temporary annexe to the town's swimming pool provided a sports hall.
As it was housed in a pressured air building, it became known as 'the bubble'. In 1986, gale force
winds caused extensive damage to various buildings, including the bubble, which was not re-opened.
(Frank Beattie)

The building above was opened as the town's Sheriff Courthouse in 1852. By the 1980s it was no longer adequate and a new Sheriff Courthouse (below) was completed in 1986 at the corner of St Marnock Street and Dundonald Road. The vacated property, almost directly across the road, became the office of the Procurator Fiscal. *(Frank Beattie)*

Kilmarnock's first custom-built theatre, the grandly named Opera House, was opened in John Finnie Street in 1875. After the closure of the theatre, the building had various uses, but in 1989 it was destroyed by fire, leaving only the façade. The site has lain derelict ever since, but ambitious plans are currently in hand to build a hotel on the premises. *(Gordon Robb)*

Kilmarnock's original public swimming pool was opened in 1940 and because of its unique wave-making machine was used for commando training during the Second World War. In 1987 the pool was replaced by the Galleon Leisure Centre, which gave the people of the area a swimming pool, ice rink for curling and skating, bowls hall, games halls and meeting rooms, as well as a restaurant and bar. *(Above and opposite bottom: Gordon Robb; opposite top: East Ayrshire Council)*

The 1980s saw the completion of the first phase of the refurbishment of the Palace Theatre, concentrating on the auditorium. Other refurbishment programmes for the theatre and the adjacent Grand Hall and Art Halls followed. *(Frank Beattie)*

The former town jail and county police station in Bank Street was demolished in 1987 to make way for a car park. This old jail was on the site of the original terminus of the Kilmarnock and Troon Railway, which operated a time-tabled passenger service from 1812. *(Frank Beattie)*

Above & below: Kilmarnock Infirmary was opened at Mount Pleasant in Wellington Street in 1868. It was extended on several occasions but closed when a replacement hospital at Crosshouse was completed. Plans for the hospital at Crosshouse were announced in 1967 and work started in 1973. The first out-patients were treated in 1981 and the first in-patients were treated in 1982.The hospital was officially opened in 1984 and has seen several changes and expansions since then. *(Author's collection and Frank Beattie)*

Kilmarnock Maternity Home was opened in the 1930s and remained in service until 1989 when services were moved to Ayrshire Central Hospital in Irvine. The picture shows the Maternity Home staff at the time of closure. *(Gordon Robb)*

Maternity services returned to Kilmarnock in 2006 when the £20 million Ayrshire Maternity Unit opened at Crosshouse Hospital to replace maternity services previously based at Ayrshire Central Hospital in Irvine. *(Frank Beattie)*

Above & below: Portland Street was at one time a prominent shopping street in the town, but a series of closures and a fire led to plans for a new shopping mall. Much of the street was cleared and it took nearly twenty years to build new shops here. *(Frank Beattie)*

Some long-established businesses did not survive the economic turmoil of the 1980s. Tam Samson opened his business in 1759 and finally closed in 1984. *(Frank Beattie)*

Other businesses have faired well against the big supermarkets by concentrating on friendly and personal service to customers. Hannah's the grocer is one such business. The shop was established in 1926 and continues to provide a service to customers today. *(Frank Beattie)*

5

1990s: The Global Village

And I think to myself 'What a wonderful world.' (George Weiss and Bob Theile)

McDonald's is a symbol of the global economy. Everyone eats the same kind of food in the same kind of places, and all in such a hurry that the products became known as fast food. *(Frank Beattie)*

Above & below: Homes and businesses in the low lying areas of Riccarton and Kilmarnock suffered flooding in 1990 and again in 1991. Then in 1994, Kilmarnock was hit by the most severe flooding in sixty years, followed by further flooding in 1995. Kilmarnock has been flooded many times over the centuries but the severity and frequency of flooding in the 1990s led to funding being found at last for flood management schemes to be put in place. *(Frank Beattie and S&UN)*

Right: Controversy surrounded the demolition in 1995 of the Glasgow, Paisley, Kilmarnock and Ayr Railway Company's station building in Kilmarnock. It had opened in 1843, but had not been used by passengers since the 1870s. *(Frank Beattie)*

Below: Another controversial demolition was that of the architecturally unique group of houses in Hood Street, known as the Walker Buildings. They had been built in 1904 by the whisky firm, Johnnie Walker, to house some of their workers and their families. *(Frank Beattie)*

Above & opposite top: The old cinema and the new. At one time Kilmarnock had seven cinemas. By the 1990s there was only one, pictured opposite above. In 1998 the Odeon cinema chain opened a new multi-screen cinema in Queen's Drive on land that had been used by Glenfield and Kennedy. The old ABC Cinema in Titchfield Street closed the following year. *(Frank Beattie)*

Eating out and going to the cinema go hand-in-hand, but once again we seem to rely on international franchises such as Pizza Hut rather than smaller independent restaurants. *(Frank Beattie)*

In a controversial move, the old red sandstone Co-op building in Portland Street was demolished in 1990. Developers promised that the façade would be retained and incorporated into the new street, but developments were delayed and when part of Portland Street was rebuilt and renamed Portland Gate, only two of the stone figures from the building were set up as artwork features in a car park at the top of the redeveloped street. *(Kilmarnock Co-op and Frank Beattie)*

A Newcomen engine was set up at Caprington Colliery in 1806 to help keep the coal pits clear of water. The cylinder came from an old engine built by the Carron Iron Company in the 1770s and worked for nearly 100 years. It was removed in 1901 and was given to the local museum, which did not have the resources to rebuild it. In 1958 it was presented to the Royal Museum of Scotland, but again no national funding was available. However, in 1998 the new Museum of Scotland was opened in Edinburgh and the Caprington Newcomen Engine at last became a major feature. *(Frank Beattie)*

The Laigh Milton Viaduct, claimed to be the oldest railway viaduct in the world, was built on the Kilmarnock and Troon Railway between 1808 and 1812. In the 1990s, amidst a clash between those who felt strongly about preserving heritage and those who did not, one success which emerged was the restoration of this viaduct. *(Frank Beattie)*

Above & below: A new fire station was opened in Titchfield Street, Kilmarnock in 1937, replacing three small units. The new station even had motorised fire engines with a novel feature – the firemen could ride inside the vehicle. These two photographs show the station and its crew shortly before the station's closure in 1994. *(Gordon Robb)*

In 1994, following the Titchfield Street fire station closure, a new station opened at Campbell Street in Riccarton. It includes a national major incident department and modern fire fighting units. The former fire station building was converted for commercial use on the ground floor, with nine homes on the upper floors, the development being called Brigade Court. *(Frank Beattie)*

The new fire station was built close to the site of Riccarton Castle which had a long association with the Wallace family. It was William Wallace who, at the close of the thirteenth century, inspired the people to resist the army of occupation. *(Frank Beattie)*

A new use was found for the former Maternity Home which closed in 1989. In 1991, the Strathlea Resource Centre for people with mental health problems was opened in the building at Holmes Road. The complex, under the auspices of Ayrshire and Arran Health Board, was the first of its kind in Scotland and provides residential accommodation for up to sixty-five people. *(Frank Beattie)*

Another fine building which was saved and given a new use was the Tech in Elmbank Avenue. This was originally the Kilmarnock Technical School and was later incorporated fully into the adjacent Kilmarnock Academy. When the building was no longer required for education in the 1990s, it was converted to flats with the name Academy Apartments. *(Frank Beattie)*

Above: Another of the industrial casualties was Craigend Mill, which was housed in a building with unusual curving walls to match the curve in the river. The building was demolished and the site was used for housing. *(Frank Beattie)*

Right: In 1991 Kilmarnock celebrated the 400th anniversary of the town having burgh status. Events included the creation of commemorative tapestries and the launch of a commemorative Kilmarnock 400 blend of whisky from the makers of Johnnie Walker. *(East Ayrshire Council)*

Above & below: Whisky makers Johnnie Walker launched a new blends for special purposes. Above, local MP Willie McKelvey inspects one of the first bottles of Gold Lable whisky, whilst below, Provost Jim Mills checks a bottle of Kilmarnock 400, launched to mark the town's 400th anniversary of having burgh status. *(Diageo)*

A ten pin bowling alley was opened in Grange Street in 1994 in property which had been used for car sales since 1931. The bowling alley took the name of The Garage. *(Frank Beattie)*

In 1993 Bellfield became the latest area of the town to get a new community centre. The building provides a venue in the community for sports, meetings and other functions. *(Frank Beattie)*

Dunn Mews: In 1991 Annanhill House was sold by the district council to property developers. Work started almost immediately on the conversion of the main building into flats. Other houses were soon constructed close to the mansion. *(Frank Beattie)*

St Andrew's Hostel, a new facility for the temporarily homeless, was opened by East Ayrshire Council in St Andrew Street in 1998. *(Frank Beattie)*

In the 1990s major refurbishment work was carried out around the Cross. This involved repaving the area with cobblestones and providing matching benches throughout the area. *(Frank Beattie)*

In addition to revamping benches in the town centre, new items commemorating town twinning were erected which included a granite plaque marking the town's twinning with Kulmbach in Germany and a statue showing figures wrapped in a map of the world. *(Frank Beattie)*

Left: Kilmarnock was twinned with the Black Sea town of Sukhumi (later Sukhum) in 1985. The collapse of the Soviet Union led to civil war in some of the former USSR states and in 1994, a memorial stone and garden were erected in Howard Park in memory of those people from Sukhumi who were killed in the conflict between Abkhazia and Georgia between 1991 and 1993. *(Frank Beattie)*

New statues and works of art were commissioned for the town centre area. These included statues of Johnnie Walker, founder of the vast whisky empire, in John Dickie Street (right), Robert Burns and his printer, John Wilson, at the Cross (below) and a stylised man reading the *Kilmarnock Standard* in Bank Street (below right). *(Frank Beattie)*

In 1997 Kilmarnock Football Club won the Scottish Cup, thus providing a great boost in the confidence of the club and in the town itself. *(Frank Beattie)*

Like most other football teams in the country, Kilmarnock Football Club's fortunes seem to vary from week to week, but match days at Rugby Park always attract a good crowd. *(Frank Beattie)*

This rather anonymous building was one of those demolished during the development of land at Queen's Drive. It was only ever described as 'a government store.' *(Frank Beattie)*

No anchor store could be found for the redeveloped Portland Street. Instead, the two big attractions were a super-sized pub and a super-sized bingo hall. *(Frank Beattie)*

6

The New Millennium

It's coming yet, for a' that,
That man to man the world o'er
Shall brothers be for a' that.

(Robert Burns)

The Dick Institute was opened in 1901 as a cultural centre for the Kilmarnock area. It housed the town's library, art gallery and museum, and still does so today. In 2007 a stone cleaning programme was completed, returning the building to its visual magnificence of early days. *(Frank Beattie)*

In the year 2000 the congregations of the West High Church in Portland Street and the Laigh Kirk in Bank Street agreed to merge under the name of the Laigh West High and to use the Laigh Kirk building. The West High Church building was converted for commercial use and took on the name of the West Kirk. *(Frank Beattie)*

Laigh Kirk. There has been a church on this site since the earliest days of the town. In 1801, panic gripped the congregation when they thought the building was falling down and in the mad rush to get out, twenty-nine people died and another died later. After that the building was taken down and a new one was constructed. *(Frank Beattie)*

Another building to be given the restoration treatment was the Old High Kirk. The building's construction was completed in 1732, though the tower was added later. A restoration programme aimed at removing later stonework treatment and restoring the eighteenth-century look was completed in 2007. *(Frank Beattie)*

The new millennium was a time of change for several church buildings. In 2003, the Sovereign Grace Church building at the junction of Fowlds Street and Old Mill Road was closed and put up for sale. The church, which had been used for worship since 1857, was soon converted into a tanning salon. *(Frank Beattie)*

St Andrew's Church was opened in 1841. In 1967, the congregations of Glencairn Church at Glencairn Square and St Andrew's Church in St Andrew Street agreed to be united under the title of St Andrew's Glencairn Church. They used the St Andrew's Church building for worship, which closed in 2002 and was converted into flats. *(Frank Beattie)*

Above & below: In 2005 house building work started on the construction of houses at Trinity Park, Fisher Grange and Alder Gate. More than 200 houses were built in these areas and at the end of 2007 planning for the construction of thousands more houses for other parts of the town was in an advanced state. *(Frank Beattie)*

Two major sites in New Mill Road were used for house building in 2007. One was on the site of a joiner's yard, pictured, and the other on the site a cash and carry warehouse. *(Frank Beattie)*

Land around Moorfield on the edge of Kilmarnock became available for housing and various house builders have moved in to construct a substantial number of new homes there. Nature conservation has influenced the overall design and this artificial pond, below, was created to help attract wildlife. *(Frank Beattie)*

Shopping continued to change in the new millennium as the big supermarkets moved to all-day opening, allowing customers to buy most products twenty-four hours a day, seven days a week, though they do close for Christmas and New Year. *(Frank Beattie)*

Charity shops also changed and became bigger and more professional. At one time the charities took small shops that were difficult to let. Now they moved into bigger properties. This one was originally built as a supermarket. *(Frank Beattie)*

There was a stushie when Morrisons were building their first Scottish supermarket in Kilmarnock. At the time, Safeway were planning to replace their Kilmarnock store. Land was cleared and planning permission given. In the meantime, Morrisons took over Safeway. The Morrisons supermarket, already under construction at West Langlands Street, was opened in 2004. The existing Safeway store was closed and their plans for a new store were dropped. In 2008, at the time of writing, Tesco have plans for their biggest Scottish store on the site previously earmarked for a new Safeway. *(Frank Beattie)*

With supermarket wars going on at a furious rate, it's nice to know that there is still room for small businesses with their traditional service. In 2007, the Forum Café celebrated seventy years of providing quality ice cream. The Forum also continues to serve the new generation with a selection of traditional sweets. Here their ice cream is being enjoyed by Kerry Dick and Rosie Beattie. The extra ice cream is for the photographer! *(Frank Beattie)*

In 2005 Powerleague came to Kilmarnock. The group has dozens of five-a-side football centres across the country. In Kilmarnock, they converted the former Kirkstyle cricket ground after the cricket club moved to new accommodation. *(Frank Beattie)*

Kilmarnock town centre is now becoming a vibrant place, with public spaces being used by entertainers and street musicians as well as for children's entertainment. *(Frank Beattie)*

Left: The Bentinck Studio was opened by Centrestage Music Theatre in James Little Street in 2006. Facilities include a fully equipped theatre, rehearsal rooms and backstage facilities to provide tuition in all aspects of music theatre for all ages. *(Frank Beattie)*

Below: The decline of heavy industry and a new awareness of the need to protect the environment have brought a new lease of healthier life for the rivers around town. This in turn has led to a new interest in angling. *(Frank Beattie)*

In 2005, the M77 motorway from Meiklewood at the north of Kilmarnock to Newton Mearns in the south of Glasgow was opened. It had first been suggested in 1974 when the Kilmarnock by-pass was opened. The new section of M77 gave people in the Kilmarnock area a direct link to Glasgow city centre and access to Scotland's motorway network. The decision to go ahead with the road gave an immediate boost to house building in the Kilmarnock area. The 9½ mile road cost £130m, and came about following intense public pressure on government. *(Frank Beattie)*

In sharp contrast to the modern motorway system, there are still a few fords around the area. Fortunately, this driver eventually realised that the river was in flood and backed off. *(Frank Beattie)*

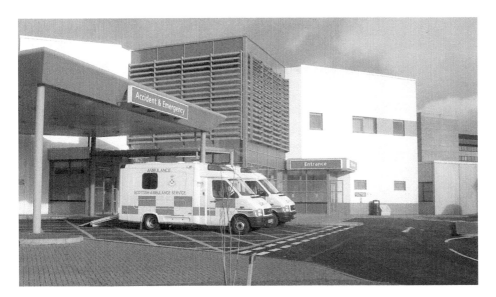

Health Minister Malcolm Chisholm officially opened the new accident and emergency extension to Crosshouse Hospital in 2004. Plans to centralise all of Ayrshire's accident and emergency services at Crosshouse were approved, but proved to be a political hot potato and were suspended then axed by the new Scottish government in 2007. *(Frank Beattie)*

A new North West Primary Care Neighbourhood Services Centre was completed in 2006 at a cost of £9m. The development was a partnership between East Ayrshire Council and NHS Ayrshire and Arran. The centre provides a variety of health and council services, including mental health services, community nurses, dementia day care, a dental surgery, dieticians, GP practice, housing team, the Hunter Sports Centre, learning disability service, midwives, occupational therapy, physiotherapy, podiatry, social work and speech and language therapy. *(Frank Beattie)*

Many new housing estates and retail developments are designed with the car in mind and despite efforts by the government to persuade us to walk more and use public transport, car sales continue to boom. *(Frank Beattie)*

In 2002 a major new development of shops was completed in Armour Street and Titchfield Street on land that had been vacant for a number of years. *(Frank Beattie)*

The Park Hotel was opened in 2002 on ground adjacent to Rugby Park football ground. It quickly gained a reputation for being one of the finest in the area. *(Frank Beattie)*

Many traditions are upheld and in the new millennium the town still manages to find land to host a traditional travelling circus. However, a recent spat between the local authority and the circus operators over the use of performing animals meant that the elephant had to miss the 2007 show in Kilmarnock. *(Frank Beattie)*

Since the new millennium, Kilmarnock has taken a new interest in the heritage of the area. Kilmarnock and District History Group, with the help of East Ayrshire Council, have placed more than thirty heritage plaques around the town, marking people, places and events of significance to the area. *(Frank Beattie)*

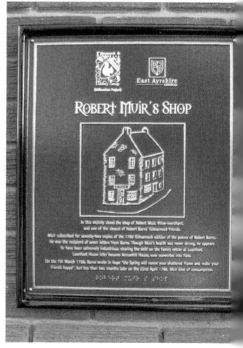

Above & below: There are two Rowallan Castles. The earlier one, above, dates from the fourteenth century and was occupied until the first decade of the twentieth century when it was replaced by New Rowallan, currently being turned into a top-rate hotel and visitor centre. In the grounds, a new world-class golf course is planned; Europe's first nineteen-hole course, with the nineteenth to be used to settle tied matches. The course, designed by top golfer Colin Montgomerie, is expected to be completed in 2008. *(James Page and Gordon Robb)*

The River Irvine marked the boundary not just between Kilmarnock and Riccarton, but between Cunninghame and Kyle. The old Riccarton Bridge was built in 1726. In 2004, the bridge was strengthened and the parapet heightened. *(Frank Beattie)*

Rowallan Creamery was established to the north of Kilmarnock by John Wallace as a 'butterine' factory in 1886. It later produced leading brands such as Banquet Margarine. The creamery closed in 2003 and the buildings were demolished to make way for forty houses. *(Frank Beattie)*

Above & below: John M. Kelso opened his paint and wallpaper shop in Queen Street in 1929, and in 1959 the business moved to Titchfield Street. The business remained there until 2004, when it moved to the Forge Industrial Estate off West Langlands Street and became known as Kelso House to Home. At that time, the business was run by the third generation of the family. The move did not pay off and the business closed in 2007. *(John Kelso and Frank Beattie)*

Above & below: St Joseph's school was moved from Elmbank Avenue to Grassyards Road in 1955. The school had been in Elmbank Avenue since 1902. The primary department remained at Elmbank Avenue and became St Columba's RC Primary School. Now, as part of East Ayrshire Council's school building programme, a new St Joseph's school building opened in 2008, adjacent to the old one. The new building also houses the primary feeder schools of St Columba's and St Matthew's which were merged to form a new St Andrew's RC Primary School. *(Frank Beattie)*

Above & below: The two buildings of St Columba's Primary School will soon be surplus to the requirements of the educational department, but, at the time of writing, no plans have been announced regarding the future of the buildings. *(Frank Beattie)*

Another school soon to get a new building is Grange Academy. The new building will incorporate Annanhill Primary School and Park School.
(Frank Beattie)

One of the most innovative house programmes in the area has been the conversion of former railway and engineering works into flats. The former Barclay railway works at West Langlands Street were converted by local firm Klin Developments. Barclay House includes a railway heritage centre and houses Drake, an industrial locomotive built in Kilmarnock by Andrew Barclay Sons and Company. *(Frank Beattie)*

Hundreds of new houses have been built in and around the town. From major developments like those at Moorfield and Mount Pleasant (pictured above), to smaller ones like London Gate, the years 2006–2007 saw an unprecedented house building programme, including 360 homes at Moorfield; 44 at New Mill Road; 138 at Deansgate; 90 homes at Mount Pleasant off Wellington Street and nearly 200 homes are planned for the site of the former carpet factory off. Barbadoes Road. The current district plan calls for another 7,000 homes to be built in the district by 2017 and more land to be released for housing. *(Frank Beattie)*

Above & Opposite: The Burns Monument in the Kay Park was built in 1879 and quickly became an icon for the town. The monument was severely damaged by a fire started by vandals in 2004. Prior to its destruction, it had been closed to the public, fenced off and neglected. Plans to build a new centre round the remains of the monument were quickly in place, but an idea of using it to house the registrar's office was controversial. A change of political administration in May 2007 brought the idea of using the building as a museum and a centre for family and local history research. *(Author's collection)*

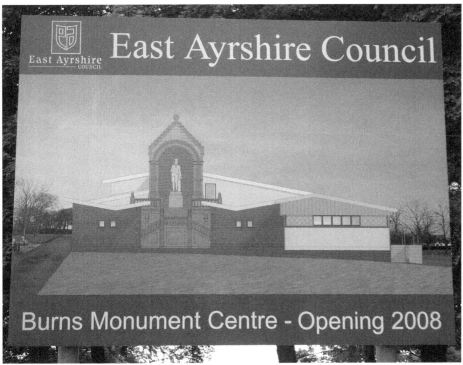

In 2007 work started on the construction of 138 houses, social housing and low cost home ownership for the first phase of a development at Longpark Avenue, Northcraig Road and Kirn Road. The development was launched under the name of Deansgate. *(Frank Beattie)*

The site of a former petrol station in London Road was used to build new flats in 2007, the development being called London Gate. *(Frank Beattie)*

7

The Future

We do not inherit the earth from our fathers. We borrow it from our children. (David Bower)

It's not just houses that are revitalising the town. Plans are in hand for the construction of an office block called Top of the Town, which will provide 46,000 square feet of new office space. *(Frank Beattie)*

Above & below: In the second half of 2007, East Ayrshire Council launched a vigorous campaign aimed at clearing the town of buildings which had been derelict for years. The site of the former cattle market and the adjacent part of West Langlands Street will soon be cleared to make way for nearly 100 flats. *(Frank Beattie)*

This building in Dunlop Street has been derelict for years, but could soon get a new lease of life as the local authority pursues a tough programme of enforcement orders and compulsory purchase orders. *(Frank Beattie)*

Derelict property in High Glencairn Street is set to be cleared. These buildings and the adjacent land are earmarked for Scotland's biggest Tesco Extra supermarket. *(Frank Beattie)*

The massive former whisky bond has had a good number of occupants on the ground floor, and currently, ambitious plans are being implemented to convert the rest of the building for use as offices and shops. *(Frank Beattie)*

The railway line from Kilmarnock to Glasgow was made a single track more than a generation ago. Work will soon begin to provide what the railway operators call a 'dynamic loop', allowing a half-hour service between Kilmarnock and Glasgow and making the station a busier place than it is in this photograph. *(Frank Beattie)*

In the new millennium everyone, it seems, wanted to get fit, a trend that is almost certain to grow. The Fitness First gym was opened in 2002. *(James Page)*

On the evening of Thursday 21 June 2007, more than an inch of rain fell in less than half an hour and caused the partial collapse of a roof at a row of shops, and the temporary closure of shops, a leisure centre, a cinema and many roads around the town. *(Frank Beattie)*

The new vibrancy of the town is already attracting well-known retailers. After an absence from the town for several years, River Island made a return in November 2007. *(Frank Beattie)*

With all the developments going on in and around the town, some buildings are at risk. Tentative approaches have been made on behalf of a developer to the property owners on the corner of Titchfield Street and Douglas Street. *(Frank Beattie)*

The *Kilmarnock Standard* has been reporting the local news since 1863 and long may it continue. Today, if you live outside the area and can't get your paper, you can call up an on-line version at www. kilmarnockstandard.co.uk. Today, Europe's biggest onshore windfarm at Whitelee, just outside Kilmarnock, is already producing electricity, even though the farm will not be completed until the end of 2009. House building is going on at a furious rate, and outstanding plans are in hand for a new hotel and a major supermarket, while work continues to shake off the last of the town's dirt and heavy industry image. The future is bright. *(Frank Beattie)*

Acknowledgements

With thanks: Pictures by Mike Bisset, Stewart McLaughlan, Allister MacPherson, James Page and Gordon Robb were originally taken for the *Kilmarnock Standard*.

Additional pictures and other illustrations have come from Sam Ewing, John Hall, John Kelso, Derry Martin, Bob Murray and Bill Paton. Thanks also go to Diageo (Johnnie Walker), East Ayrshire Council, Glenfield and Kennedy, Massey-Ferguson, Kilmarnock Football Club, *Kilmarnock Standard* and the Royal Bank of Scotland for permission to use illustratons.

Thanks also go to the staff at Hector McDonald's Camera House for their attention to detail in copying and scanning pictures and to staff at the reference section of the Dick Institute library for helping to find information to accompany the pictures.

About the Author

Frank Beattie was born in 1952 at Kilmarnock, Ayrshire, in the south-west of Scotland. He was educated at Bentinck Primary School, James Hamilton High School and Kilmarnock Academy. In 1972 he joined the editorial team at the *Kilmarnock Standard*. Calling on his love of local history, he began writing features on regional matters which progressed to a weekly page containing a mix of features, old photographs, queries and memories sent in by readers. At the end of 2002, he became a production editor with the same company, based in Irvine, and such was the popularity of his *Memories* page that he continues to produce this. He has also written several books on aspects of Kilmarnock's history.

Bibliography

Books

Boyle, Andrew. *Ayrshire Heritage*, Alloway Publishing, Darvel, 1990
Donnelly, Frank. *The History of Kilmarnock Academy*, Kilmarnock Academy, 1998
Douglas, James. *Scottish Banknotes*, Stanley Gibbons, 1975
Heaney, George. *Sixty Years of A1 Service*, Bus Enthusiast Publishing Company, 1991
Knox, John. *Maps of Kilmarnock 1792–1992*, Kilmarnock and District History Group, 1992
MacDonald, Neil. *The Western Way*, The Transport Publishing Company, 1983
Malkin, John. *Pictorial History of Kilmarnock*, Alloway Publishing, Darvel, 1989
McKay, Archibald and William Findlay. *History of Kilmarnock (5th edition)*, *Kilmarnock Standard*, 1909
Morgan, Mike. *Daggers Drawn: Real Heroes of the SAS and SBS*, Sutton Publishing, 2003
Murdoch, John. *A Million to One Against, A Portrait of Andrew Fisher*, Minerva Press, 1998
Starsfield, Gordon. *Ayrshire and Renfrewshire's Lost Railways*, Stenlake, 1999
Strawhorn, John. *History of Irvine*, John Donald Publishers, Edinburgh, 1985
Strawhorn, John and Andrew, Ken. *Discovering Ayrshire*, John Donald, 1988
Wear, Russell. *Barclay 150*, Hunslet Barclay, 1990

Periodicals & Other References

Ayrshire Collections, Ayrshire Archaeological and Natural History Society, 1950–1976
Ayrshire Notes, Ayrshire Federation of Historical Societies
Kilmarnock & District History Group Newsletters
Kilmarnock Standard
Kilmarnock Standard Annual
Mount House Kilmarnock, 1793–1993